The Apache Wars: The History and Legacy of the U.S. Army's Campaigns against the Apaches

By Sean McLachlan and Charles River Editors

A picture of Geronimo and a group of Apache warriors

About Charles River Editors

Charles River Editors provides superior editing and original writing services across the digital publishing industry, with the expertise to create digital content for publishers across a vast range of subject matter. In addition to providing original digital content for third party publishers, we also republish civilization's greatest literary works, bringing them to new generations of readers via ebooks.

Sign up here to receive updates about free books as we publish them, and visit Our Kindle Author Page to browse today's free promotions and our most recently published Kindle titles.

About the Author

Sean McLachlan has spent much of his life in Arizona and Missouri, working as an archaeologist and tracing legends of the Old West. Now a full-time writer, he's the author of many history books and novels, including *A Fine Likeness*, a Civil War novel with a touch of the weird. For more information, check out his Amazon page and blog.

Introduction

Geronimo in 1886

The Apache Wars

"Even if we should be able to dislodge them from the rough mountain ridges and impenetrable woods which cover the immense territories of these frontiers, they would seek better asylum in the vastness of the Sierra Madre... [They] know how to surprise and destroy our troops in the mountains and on the plains. They are not ignorant of the use and power of our arms; they manage their own with dexterity; and they are as good or better horsemen than the Spaniards, and having no towns, castles, or temples to defend they may only be attacked in their dispersed and movable rancherias." - Bernardo de Galvez, *Instructions for Governing the Interior Provinces of New Spain, 1787* (The Quivera Society, Berkeley)

The Apache of the American Southwest have achieved almost legendary status for their fierceness and their tenacity in fighting the U.S. Army. Names like Nana, Cochise, and Geronimo are synonymous with bravery and daring, and the tribe had that reputation long before the Americans arrived. Indeed, among all the Native American tribes, the Spanish, Mexicans, and Americans learned the hard way that the warriors of the Apache were perhaps the fiercest in North America. Based in the Southwest, the Apache fought all three in Mexico and the American Southwest, engaging in seasonal raids for so many centuries that the Apache struck fear into the hearts of all their neighbors.

Given the group's reputation, it's fitting that they are inextricably associated with one of their most famous leaders, Geronimo. Descendants of people killed by "hostile" Apache certainly considered warriors like Geronimo to be murderers and thieves whose cultures and societies held no redeeming values, and even today, many Americans associate the name Geronimo with a war cry. The name Geronimo actually came about because of a battle he fought against the Mexicans.

Over time, however, the historical perception of the relationship between America and Native tribes changed drastically. With that, Geronimo was viewed in a far different light, as one of a number of Native American leaders who resisted the U.S. and Mexican governments when settlers began to push onto their traditional homelands. Like the majority of Native American groups, the Apache were eventually vanquished and displaced by America's westward push, and Geronimo became an icon for eluding capture for so long.

The Apache Wars: The History and Legacy of the U.S. Army's Campaigns against the Apaches analyzes the history of the campaigns that stretched over decades. Along with pictures of important people, places, and events, you will learn about the Apache Wars like never before, in no time at all.

The Apache Wars: The History and Legacy of the U.S. Army's Campaigns against the Apaches
About Charles River Editors
About the Author
Introduction
   Chapter 1: The Origins of the Apache
   Chapter 2: The Spanish and Mexican Periods
   Chapter 3: America's Problem
   Chapter 4: The Civil War Years
   Chapter 5: Escalating Conflict
   Chapter 6: General Crook and the Beginning of the End
   Chapter 7: The Geronimo Campaign
   Online Resources
   Bibliography

Chapter 1: The Origins of the Apache

First migrating to the Southwest from western Canada sometime around 1000-1500, the Apache lived a hunting and gathering lifestyle in the rough mountains and vast stretches of desert left unused by the agricultural peoples who had preceded them, or fought for the scarce temperate highlands of the region's many mountain ranges. The Apache kept herds of animals and would trade and raid with the settled tribes.

While the origin of the name "Apache" is a point of contention among modern linguists, many believe it was derived from the Yavapai word epache, meaning "people," while also having some relationship with the Zuni word *apachu*, meaning "enemy." Another popular assertion is that "Apache" was actually the Zuni designation for the Navajo and not specifically the Apache people, because early Spanish chroniclers wrote that the Zuni name for Navajo was "Apachis de Nabaju," with "Apache" actually a Quechan word meaning "fighting-men. Today, the Apache prefer the designations *N'de, Dišnë, Tišndende, Inde,* or *Nide* (meaning "the people.")

The most widely-accepted hypothesis dates the arrival of the Apache, Navajo, and Ute to around 1500, during what is referred to as the "Dinétah" archaeological phase of the Upper San Juan River drainage area in northwestern New Mexico, southwestern Colorado, southeastern Utah, and northeastern Arizona. Another common theory contends that these groups first entered the U. S. Southwest during the Historic period after the Puebloan Revolt of 1680, when the Pueblo nations expelled Spanish colonizers and restored self-rule. Yet another theory, which is promoted by Barry Pritzker in *Native American Encyclopedia: History, Culture, and Peoples*, is that Athabaskan ancestors of the Apache and Navajo migrated into the Southwest around 1400, but physical evidence does not support this contention yet. Whatever the timing, historians consider the Apache, Navajo and Ute as relative "new arrivals" to the region, and they arrived as hunter-gatherers, establishing villages north and between Anasazi, Mogollon, and Hohokam homelands. By some reckoning, both the Apache and Navajo constitute subgroups of the Ute people, with the Apache infiltrating the Southwest and establishing themselves in the Great Basin. Other historians contend that the Ute actually arrived in the Southwest as early as 1200 and were responsible for driving out the Puebloans virtually single-handedly.

While these theories trace the Apache migration from Northwestern Canada (and perhaps Alaska) to the Southwest around 1500, some Apache groups contend that it actually occurred in reverse. They contend that around 1500 and contact with the Spanish, most Athapaskan-speaking people migrated to the North, with only a minority remaining in the Southwest. Whichever direction they came from, everyone agrees that by the end of the 1600s, about 5,000 Apache occupied the Southwest.

Once the Apache, Navajo and Ute separated from the Athabaskan-speaking group in Canada, the Apache-Navajo migrated south along the High Plains of the United States, following the outer ridge of the Rocky Mountains and passing through Montana and Nebraska. Encountering comparatively more-aggressive Plains groups like the Pawnee along the way, who at this time lived in fortified villages and conducted small-scale farming, the Apache remained more mobile, while the Navajo adopted basic farming techniques. Upon arrival in the Puebloan homelands, the Apache and Navajo began to experiment with farming, settling pueblo-like villages (building *hogans,* permanent wooden and stone structures) and raiding surrounding Puebloan settlements. It was this activity that presumably resulted in the exodus by the remaining Anasazi, Mogollon, and Hohokam.

When those groups left, the Navajo and Apache essentially divided up the Southwest territory, with the Navajo assuming control of the "Four-Corners" area and the Apache taking the mountains and plains of southern Arizona and New Mexico and northwestern Mexico. It was from there that the Apache eventually subdivided into the Arivaipa, Chiricahua, Coyotero, Faraone Gileno, Llanero, Mescalero, Mimbreno, Naisha, Tchikun, and Tchishi subgroups, but they were collectively known as a powerful and warlike people.

Chapter 2: The Spanish and Mexican Periods

Although the Spanish didn't formally mention the Apache until 1598, when Spanish Conquistador Don Juan de Oñate y Salazar entered the region, historians think it likely that Spanish explorer Francisco Vásquez de Coronado was referring to the Querecho Apache in 1541 when he described a group he encountered on the Plains of east New Mexico and west Texas. Coronado wrote, "After seventeen days of travel, I came upon a 'rancheria' of the Indians who follow these cattle. These natives are called Querechos. They do not cultivate the land, but eat raw meat and drink the blood of the cattle they kill. They dress in the skins of the cattle, with which all the people in this land clothe themselves, and they have very well-constructed tents, made with tanned and greased cowhides, in which they live and which they take along as they follow the cattle. They have dogs which they load to carry their tents, poles, and belongings."

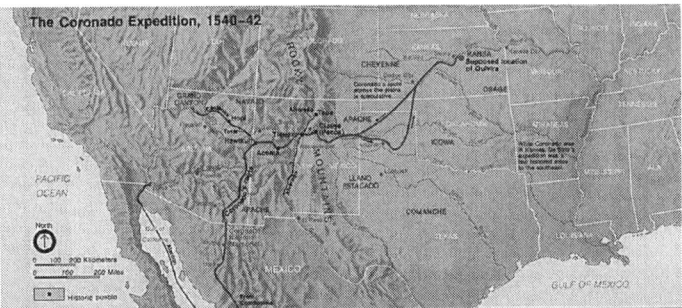

Coronado's route in red shows which Native American groups he likely encountered.

Regardless of when they encountered the Apache, the Spaniards colonized the upper Rio

Grande Valley by 1598, bringing large numbers of livestock and horses to the West and Southwest. Almost immediately, the Spanish drive northward disrupted traditional Apache trade with neighboring tribes and alerted them to possible invasion. The Apache had been trading with the Pueblo and also stealing from them during raids, and once the Pueblo began to acquire horses, the Apache quickly began taking horses and adopting Spanish cavalry tactics. Crafting leather shields and chestplates, they armed themselves with Spanish-style lances (in addition to their traditional bows and arrows) and were quickly able to assume military dominance of the region. With superior numbers the key to their former battle strategies (and one reason most Apache groups never subdivided into small bands), the Apache could now take on considerably larger forces regardless of numerical disparities. Thus, by 1650, the so-called "horse frontier" was regarded by most as "Apache Territory" and was strictly avoided unless the people entering the region were prepared for confrontation.

The Apache came to the attention of the Spanish military when they started raiding in the 1650s and then aided the great Pueblo Revolt of 1680, which for a few years pushed the Spanish out of the region. By 1710 they were making frequent and serious raids into Spanish territory, and by 1750 threatening to push the Spaniards out a second time. Settlers in outposts such as Tubac (founded 1752) and Tucson (founded 1769) cowered behind town walls at night, and were under threat whenever they ventured forth to tend their herds and fields.

It is during the early Spanish period that the Apache first encountered wild horses and for a time considered them game. At some point the Apache developed their own riding style that differed from the Spanish style, so it seems they did not learn riding from the colonists but rather by independent invention. Reports from the Pueblo Revolt of 1680 showed that the Apache had already become excellent horsemen by this early date. While the Apache adopted some elements of Spanish culture, most particularly metalworking, their traditional method of fighting was what gave them the upper hand. The Spanish were not sufficiently willing or able to adapt their fighting to the circumstances and paid the price.

The Spanish relied on far-flung and often undermanned presidio garrisons, and the occasional use of larger forces from the regular army. These forces were augmented by local militias and allied Native Americans. The supply chain was slow, often cut, and unreliable in the best of times. The Apache, on the other hand, had no supply chain. They lived off the land, had no centers of population to destroy, no capital to capture, no leaders who couldn't be replaced. The Spanish, accustomed to the European style of war, couldn't figure out a way to defeat them. When fighting the Aztecs and Inca, the Spaniards had been fighting complex civilizations like their own and enjoyed a technological superiority and numerous local allies. When fighting the Apache, they found themselves facing a hydra. Isolated victories over small bands did nothing to stop the threat from other small bands.

The main force trying to protect the provinces from the Apache was the leatherjacket soldiers.

These cavalrymen, dressed in heavy leather armor, were armed with muskets, lances, and swords. They generally used heavy cavalry tactics ill-suited to the terrain. While their firearms struck fear into tribesmen unaccustomed to facing black powder, firearms were underused due to powder shortages and the fact that the men had to pay for their own weapons. This understandably led to little gunnery practice. When the Spanish did defeat the Apache in battle, it was usually thanks to their Native American allies.

Spanish attempts to co-opt the Apache usually ended in failure. The Lipan Apache, harassed by the Comanche, asked the Spanish to build them a mission in the underpopulated area between Tejas and Nuevo Mexico in 1756. When the Comanche approached one day, the priest welcomed them inside. The Comanche slaughtered everyone and never again would the Apache request a mission be built for them.

More successful was the settling in 1760 of the Jicarilla Apache in Nuevo Mexico, where they were given metal tools and taught to farm. No attempt was made to convert them to Christianity. In 1786, the Spanish Viceroy Bernardo de Gálvez spread this policy to other bands that sued for peace to create pockets of allied natives throughout the Interior Provinces. Other groups were put on reservations, where they were supplied with food, clothing, liquor, and poor-quality firearms in exchange for their submission. The Spanish government encouraged animosity between the various groups to keep them occupied, and did nothing to improve living conditions.

There were also experiments in creating native militia. Despite having to put down a revolt of the Pima Indians in 1751, Spanish authorities recruited a company of Pima in 1782 at the San Ignacio Mission in southern Arizona. It was commanded by a Spanish lieutenant, a Spanish ensign, and two sergeants. The experiment proved successful and was soon adopted at other outposts. They were trained and equipped along Spanish lines but had the advantage of native knowledge and tracking abilities. This proved vital in frequent fights with the Apache, in which the new units often came out as the victors.

By the early 1700s, however, the landscape changed dramatically. There was a widespread abandonment of Puebloan settlements, the migration of Coyotero and other Western Apache to points west of the Rio Grande River, the unsettling consequences of the Puebloan Revolt of 1690, and an influx of armed Comanche into Apache territories. The Comanche were superior fighters and superior raiders who frequently led successful horse-raiding missions against the Apache. All of this resulted in forcing the displacement of Apache groups. For example, the Lipan and various other Apache were forced to move south to follow their main food source (the buffalo), and there were at least seven different Native American groups now competing for resources. The displaced Apache, as well as the Suma, Jocomes, Janos, and Manso (all of whom were labeled "hostile Apache" by the Spanish) began raiding for food, and their economic structure shifted from mostly bison hunting to a raiding-hunting combination.

Apache raids on white settlements became an even bigger factor as whites pushed into the region, and the European powers also made frequent alliances to fight each other as well. The French supplied guns to indigenous groups of the Northwest, and the Spanish armed the Navajo, Ute, and Comanche. This also meant that Apache raids soon included the taking of firearms, powder and balls, and metal tools, as well as European shirts, trousers, vests, and hats. Within a century, traditional Apache garb had completely given way to white clothes. The Spanish also introduced slavery to the Apache by capturing and trading people or purchasing them as captives from other frontier groups. In time, Apache raids also took slaves along with the livestock and weaponry.

Unsurprisingly, the Apache were hostile to the whites who came in contact with them, and the Apache were considered a big enough problem that several European nations intended to colonize the region and round up the Apache onto reservations. In 1787, the Viceroy of "New Spain", the name given to Spanish-claimed North American territory, began sending Spanish cavalry to attack Apache settlements and demand that they settle near Spanish frontier military posts, where they would receive food, liquor, and be permitted to trade. While most Apache resisted, some preferred reservation life to war, like the White Mountain Apache. Meanwhile, the Spanish governor of New Mexico, Colonel Juan Bautista de Anza, imposed a policy disallowing trade between the Apache and Navajo, while also allying with the Comanche and Ute. This served to further divide those Apache groups under Spain's watchful eye from those that were not. As ethnographer Ernest Wallace explains in *The Comanches*, "The two [Apache and Comanche] became implacable foes...and warfare prevailed between the two tribes most of the time to 1875. On the plains the Comanches were victorious, but in the hills and mountains the Apaches were able to resist successfully."

Portrait of de Anza

By the 1790s, the Spanish had armed the native militia with guns and were employing Apache scouts. Records are sparse, but their efforts clearly helped reopen the trade route between Sonora and New Mexico, which had been cut off by hostile Apaches a century earlier.

This worked until 1810, when supplies dried up thanks to the economic and political deterioration of the empire. When this happened, the natives rebelled. By the time Mexico achieved independence in 1821, the region had been all but lost. The Mexicans started putting more pressure on the region in the ensuing decades but their control was tenuous at the best of times.

The central government Mexico City, occupied with numerous power struggles, considered its northernmost province of Sonora as a low priority. In 1821 it had a widely dispersed population of barely 50,000. Few soldiers were stationed there and they were underfed, underequipped, and underpaid. Many were conscripted convicts hauled from jail cells and banished to the wilderness. As in the Spanish period, civilians in communities such as Tucson relied on walls to protect them. Those ranchers, farmers, and miners left outside the walls had to fend for themselves. Not even the walls always worked. While the Tucsonans managed to fight off every attack, Apaches managed to sneak over the walls of Fronteras several times between 1832 and 1849, killing some 200 civilians.

Those soldiers who were stationed in the north either occupied the main towns or a series of nine presidios, of which Tucson was one, each manned by a hundred troops and three to five commissioned officers. While these small garrisons managed to launch some successful campaigns against hostile bands, they couldn't hope to stop all the small raiding groups that went south to attack the richer spoils in the province of Chihuahua.

By 1830, most Apache who strove to retain independence were driven to raiding (particularly of Northern Piman and Opata settlements), and they made frequent forays into Mexico. Generations of Apache had taken part in Mexican raids, and they thoroughly understood Mexican military tactics, knew the Mexican landscape intimately, and had come to favor Mexican women as concubines and sex captives. In fact, there were noted physical differences among various Apache groups by the early 19th century, and these differences were largely due to Apache-Mexican interaction.

In both the Spanish and Mexican periods, the government offered a bounty for scalps. In the 1830s, the price was 100 pesos for the scalp of any warrior aged fourteen or over. Fifty pesos were paid for female scalps, and 25 for a child's. As an added bounty, the scalper got to keep whatever he took from the Apaches, even if it had been originally taken from a Mexican. Many Apaches have asserted that they didn't have a tradition of scalping until the Spanish introduced it. Apaches have an aversion to the dead, avoiding burial grounds and the sites of old battles. While they sometimes mutilated their enemies in the belief that the way a person died would be how they lived in the afterlife, keeping a scalp would be considered unclean.

As a result, when the United States took over much of the Apache's land after the Mexican-American War, they inherited Mexico's problem with the Apache. From 1848-1886, the U.S. would find itself embroiled in a bloody and frustrating war with North America's fiercest tribe.

Chapter 3: America's Problem

In 1848, a victorious United States forced Mexico to sign the Treaty of Guadalupe Hidalgo, ending the Mexican-American war. The United States gained 525,000 square miles of land, including California, New Mexico, Arizona, Nevada, Utah, and parts of Wyoming and Colorado. A key section of the treaty read, "Considering that a great part of the territories, which, by the present treaty, are to be comprehended for the future within the limits of the United States, is now occupied by savage tribes, who will hereafter be under the exclusive control of the Government of the United States, and whose incursions within the territory of Mexico would be prejudicial in the extreme, it is solemnly agreed that all such incursions shall be forcibly restrained by the Government of the United States whensoever this may be necessary; and that when they cannot be prevented, they shall be punished by the said Government, and satisfaction for the same shall be exacted all in the same way, and with equal diligence and energy, as if the same incursions were meditated or committed within its own territory, against its own citizens."

While this section of the treaty was negated by the Gadsden Treaty of 1854, both sides felt it important that the other try to stop Apaches from raiding over the border, and their repeated failure to do so would be a constant source of tensions between the two nations. Numerous times, the Apache were able to elude pursuit by crossing a border for which they, having been in the land first, had no respect. At the height of the Apache wars, Mexico and the United States did make an agreement to allow troops in hot pursuit to cross the border, but a clear agreement was never communicated to the people on the ground, and much misunderstanding and mistrust resulted.

At first the Apache were relatively friendly to the Americans, hoping they would be better neighbors than the scalp-taking Mexicans. Relations soon turned sour, however, as raiding led to American reprisals and tensions escalated. Another factor was gold prospecting. The Apache thought of gold as holy. It was the only metal that wasn't, in their view, useful for anything and thus belonged to the god Ussen. To dig it up was considered sacrilege and the cause of earthquakes and other natural disasters.

The influx of whites into New Mexico Territory (what is now New Mexico and Arizona) in the 1850s led to a decline of game and available rangeland. Skirmishes between settlers and Apaches became common and some citizens groups took matters into their own hands and set out parties to hunt them down.

The U.S. Army was stretched thin, with only a few scattered forts manned mostly by Dragoons armed with single-shot muskets and almost no artillery. These Dragoons roved through the desert and mountains of the Southwest, chasing after bands of hostile Apache and other tribes. While they had some success, the natives knew the land far better than they did and found it easy to disappear into the deep canyons and rough mountains and elude pursuit.

All the while, the Apache were only one of many tribes in Arizona, New Mexico, western Texas, and northern Mexico. Some of the more settled groups, such as the Pima and Zuni, soon came to terms with the settlers, being more accustomed to trading than raiding and having more in common with the settlers thanks to their economies based on agriculture and herding. Not surprisingly, many of these groups were not so friendly themselves. The Navajo, although an agricultural people, fought an on-and-off war with the Americans from 1846-1864 to defend their land against encroachments from the whites, while the Zuni and Utes allied themselves with the whites. Another hostile group was the Walapai, who had a bitter fight with the whites until 1868, when they were finally defeated and forced onto a reservation.

One cause of hostilities was American lack of understanding of how Native American government worked. Chiefs were not absolute rulers; there was a greater or lesser degree of freedom in all tribes, and chiefs, while respected, did not have to be obeyed completely. When Americans signed treaties with friendly chiefs, they thought the chiefs would impose the treaty as a new law on their people, when all the chief could actually do was try to use his charisma and influence to convince his people to cooperate. There were always young warriors eager for loot and action who would continue raiding. When this happened, the Americans felt the chiefs had broken the treaty and would then attack the entire tribe. This, of course, would lead to hostility from formerly friendly people who felt they were being punished for the actions of others. Often the friendly chiefs would try to calm matters by making another treaty, which again be broken by warlike members of their tribe, starting the cycle again. Each cycle would make things worse for the tribe, with greater expeditions sent against them, more loss of life, land, and property, and a harsher treaty at the end of it.

This is what happened with the Navajo, who signed the Bear Springs Treaty in 1846, making peace with the Americans. The peace was almost immediately broken by young warriors and led to a cycle of war and peacemaking that ended with the starving and defeated Navajo being force-marched onto a reservation in 1864.

The difficulty in making treaties was even more marked with the Apache, who, unlike their agricultural cousins, were hunters and gatherers, living in small bands rarely numbering over 200 and often numbering much less. In their case, a chief had only nominal control over his own band, and no control over other bands. Thus a treaty with the Tonto wouldn't be honored or perhaps even known about by the Jicarilla.

Matters escalated with the Apache in 1854 when they handed the U.S. Army one of its worst defeats of the Apache Wars. In the spring of that year, there were numerous raids around northern New Mexico in the vicinity of the town of Cieneguilla. On March 5, a band of Jicarilla Apache under Chief Lobo clashed with a company of U.S. Dragoons from Fort Union. They managed to kill two Dragoons but got the worst of the fight by losing five, including Chief Lobo. The Apaches then circled around and attacked the fort's herd of cattle, taking 200 of them.

When a large band of Jicarilla was spotted in the mountains near Cieneguilla, settlers and Dragoons alike assumed these were the same band, so Lt. John Davidson led 60 Dragoons out to find them on March 30 and tracked them down to a large rancheria on a wooded ridge. There were some 100-130 warriors and a greater number of women and children. Spotting the Dragoons approaching up the canyon leading to the ridge, the Apache hurried their women and children out of harm's way and waited for the soldiers in their camp, it being an easily defended point. The Apache shouted at and mocked the soldiers as they appeared. Lt. Davidson showed poor tactics by tethering his horses at the base of the ridge in some low ground and leaving only a few men to guard them. He then took the rest of his command and charged up the steep slope. He soon came under fire, but he and his men quickly gained the summit and drove the Apache out of the camp.

As it turned out, the Apache retreat was feigned. They encircled Lt. Davidson's command and swept down the ridge to hit the horse holders. Soon the isolated rearguard was completely cut off and taking fire from all sides. The main force was in the Apache camp only about five minutes before they had to hurry back to save horse holders and were themselves surrounded. Private

James Strowbridge remembered this phase of the fight:

> "The Indians in a moment, or two, made a charge on us from three sides at once. We repulsed them again & were then ordered to screen ourselves behind any trees or breastwork that we could get. We surrounded the horses in a sort of circle, and while in that position the Indians made two more charges on us from three sides at once. We drove them back each time.
>
> "There was some times 20 minutes, some times half an hour, elapsed between these charges. Afterwards they would charge together from, some times one side, & some times another. The men from one side, would go to the other where the Indians were charging to assist in repelling them. We repulsed them every time. We fought at that place from an hour and a half, to two hours, we lost some men there and killed some Indians. I saw two Indians fall myself."

Losing men and horses at an alarming rate, Lt. Davidson ordered his men to cut their way out of the trap. They first hurried to a nearby hill, which proved too exposed, and then up to a nearby ridge that offered a way out. Sergeant James Bronson later reported, "The moment we reached the summit of the mountain [ridge], they attacked us, there, there was an engagement of ten minutes. The command after this engagement changed its direction to the left, we were then moving on the ridge of a mountain. We had moved but 20 or 30 rods from when we had our first engagement, on top of the mountain, when the Indians attacked us in rear. "The wounded men were then placed with the horses & the others defended the flanks & rear. We moved slowly on in that manner for nearly half a mile, being attacked several times by the Indians, in going that distance but they were repelled each time by the soldiers."

The Dragoons took heavy losses as they retreated along the ridge and then into a nearby ravine. Private Strowbridge was one of the lucky ones and was still alive and well. He reported:

> "I can not recollect the number of times we faced about to meet and repel the Indians, but the last time we faced about was just before we went down on the other side of the hill. We kept our position there for near twenty minutes, I think, fighting the Indians, intending to hold the position. I was sitting behind a tree trying to get a shot at an Indian, a shot struck the ground by my side, and another passed between Private Newhand's legs as he was squatting down, he said it wasn't best for us to stay there as we were not sheltered. The Indians at this time commenced firing arrows very fast, you could see fifteen or twenty falling on the ground at once. As we raised up to change our position I heard some body say that the Lieutenant was wounded. I turned around and saw an arrow sticking in his shoulder, he said never mind it is nothing. Corporal Dempsey, I think, pulled the arrow out, the Capt. was wounded himself through the leg by a ball, & one of his thumbs was shot in two.

"About this time Sergt. Holbrook came walking along by me, and asked me if I could get him a horse, he said I am shot and can not go any further on foot. I got him a horse and he tried to mount, but he was so weak he couldn't. He was very bloody, he had two arrows sticking in him, one in his back nearly to the feathers. When he tried to mount the horse, he fell over backwards & died. I can not tell how long afterwards we stayed at this place. This was the last fight that we made. Capt. Davidson gave the command then to mount and forward and we moved down the hill. There were but few left who were not wounded. We put the wounded men on the horses, a wounded man on a horse, and a well man behind him, we retreated in that manner from the field."

Once the Dragoons made it down the ravine, the Apache tired of the fight and let them go. In this, the soldiers were fortunate; they had lost 22 killed, 23 wounded, and most of their horses, but if the Apache had pressed them, they might have wiped them out entirely. Reports of the number of Jicarilla killed range from 2-50.

Subsequent investigation proved the group the Dragoons fought were not the hostile band of Jicarilla and had not been engaged in raiding but rather in making *ollas*, a type of waterproof jug they traded with the Mexicans. While they hadn't been hostile before the battle, they were, of course, hostile afterwards. The Battle of Cieneguilla led to a long campaign against the Jicarilla that ended with their being placed on a reservation, but time and again, cases of mistaken identity increased the bitterness and mistrust between the settlers and the natives.

A picture of the part of the battleground of the Battle of Cieneguilla

Chapter 4: The Civil War Years

During the American Civil War from 1861-1865, the Southwest was drained of troops to fight the big battles against each other, so many of the already undermanned garrisons were left with barely a third of their troops. The Apache took advantage of this to launch bold and widespread raids.

Civilians tried to fight back by forming ad hoc militias, but these tended to be amateurish outfits. One exception was the militia organized by King Woolsey, a rancher and prospector who once mixed pinole with strychnine and gave it to a group of Indians. Woolsey led three major operations against Apaches through some of the roughest terrain in the region. Woolsey hated the Apaches but understood them. After fighting off a raiding group at his ranch on the Gila River about 80 miles north of Yuma, he hung the body of an Apache he had killed on a tree as a warning to others, thus playing on the Apache fear of dead bodies. It worked.

Woolsey

On his raids, he went with large groups of well-armed and mounted men along with pack animals and brought back loot and scalps. One interesting note from Woolsey himself in 1864 was that he discovered the Tonto and Pinal Apache were making arrows in the style of the Mohave and Yavapai, hoping to fool the whites into thinking those generally friendly tribes were doing the raiding. Woolsey is also notable for his early advocacy for using Indians, including Apaches, as scouts.

Woolsey was prescient in another way. In an 1864 report to Territorial Governor John Goodwin, he wrote, "We have followed the trail of the Apache to his home in the mountains, and have learned where it is located. We have dispelled the idea of vast numbers that has ever attached to that tribe. A few hundred of poor miserable wretches compose the formidable foe so much dreaded by many. They will be brought to terms speedily, or exterminated, I cannot doubt, when once the government shall know how small is the enemy by which so much annoyance has been caused." Woolsey had realized that the Americans' ever-increasing numbers would one day seal the Apaches' fate.

Fighting between the government and the Apaches, especially the Chiricahua, continued throughout the Civil War years. One of the leaders, Mangas Coloradas, was well known to the Americans, having made a treaty with them as far back as 1852. At that time, the war leader was known for his bitter raids across the border into Mexico. During the 1852 negotiation, Mangas was asked why he continued to fight against the Mexicans while making terms with the Americans. He replied, "I will tell you. Some time ago my people were invited to a feast; aguardiente, or whiskey, was there; my people drank and became intoxicated, and were lying asleep, when a party of Mexicans came in and beat out their brains with clubs. At another time a trader was sent among us from Chihuahua. While innocently engaged in trading. . .a cannon concealed behind the goods was fired upon my people, and quite a number were killed. . .How can we make a peace with such a people!"

Indeed, the Mexicans tried numerous ruses to kill off the Apache. Time and again bands of Apache would be lured into Mexican towns with the promise of trade and booze, only to be set upon once they were intoxicated. Even Geronimo once fell for this trick and barely escaped with his life. The men would always be killed, and the women and children sold into slavery, so while there were periods when the Apaches tried to come to terms with the Americans, they always held bitterness in their hearts against the Mexicans for their double-dealing and trading in scalps.

Peace with the Americans was no simple matter either. The 1852 treaty went the way of so many treaties, made obsolete by the hotheads on both sides. Mangas' main ally was Cochise, who alternated between fighting and trading with the newcomers. From 1860-1861, the chief had a contract with the Butterfield Stage Line to supply wood to its station at Apache Pass. Nearby was a ranch owned by John Ward and his Mexican common law wife Jesusa Martinez. In late 1860, a band of Apaches, probably Pinals, raided the ranch, stole some livestock, and made away with Ward's twelve-year-old son Felix. It was common for Apache to capture children, whom they would raise as Apache to replace those who had been killed in raids.

A bronze bust of Cochise

Suspicion was laid on Cochise, who was asked on February 4, 1861 to meet with Second Lieutenant George Bascom to discuss the matter. Cochise arrived with a few followers to find Bascom camped with 54 soldiers and an interpreter. Seeing such numbers must have put Cochise on edge, but nevertheless he joined Bascom in his tent. Cochise insisted that it wasn't his band that had taken the boy, but Bascom didn't believe him and told the chief that he was under arrest until Felix was returned. Cochise then whipped out a knife, cut out the back of the tent, pushed through the cordon of soldiers surrounding it, and ran off, sped on his way by a hail of rifle fire.

This led to war. Cochise raided the stagecoach station and wagon trains and had several skirmishes with troops. Soon both sides had hostages and Cochise and Bascom made tentative plans for a prisoner exchange and a renewal of peace. The arrival of a large body of army reinforcements in Apache Pas, however, made Cochise suspect more treachery. He killed his prisoners and disappeared into the mountains. The army, in turn, killed their prisoners, which included three of Cochise's relatives.

Cochise subsequently went on a rampage, killing 150 whites in the next two months, and the fighting would continue throughout the war. The most brutal engagement was the Battle of Apache Pass. In 1862, a column of Union troops from California entered the New Mexico Territory (which comprised what is now Arizona and New Mexico) in order to push out a small rebel force of Texans who had claimed it for the Confederacy. As the California column moved eastwards, their worst opposition came not from the Confederates but from the Apache, who had grown bold since the frontier forts had been abandoned by the rebels and not yet reoccupied by Union troops.

Apache Pass

The column was composed of the 2nd California Cavalry, 1st California Infantry, artillery battery of two twelve-pounder mountain guns, and civilian teamsters (including future Tombstone sheriff Johnny Behan). Two Chiricahua Apache war leaders, Mangas Coloradas and Cochise, saw them coming and hit upon a plan. The column would have to pass for more than 24 hours across a scorching alkali plain on which no water could be found until making it to Apache Pass. This pass had water, but the springs were dominated by steep cliffs. The Chiricahua had long experience fighting the Americans and were armed with percussion cap muskets and rifles just like their opponents. The California troops, on the other hand, had little or no battle experience.

As a result, Apache Pass was an important strategic point. It was the only reliable source of water within 30-40 miles to the east or west, and it was a stop for the Butterfield Overland Stagecoach. If the soldiers could be denied Apache Pass, the entire column would be in danger of dying of thirst.

The advance column arrived at the pass around noon on July 15, 1862 after a baking march through the Arizona summer sun. Captain John C. Cremony, who commanded the cavalry escort guarding the supply wagons on the expedition, wrote about the battle in his memoir *Life among the Apaches*. He related how the Apaches let the advance part of the column led by Captain Thomas Roberts reach two-thirds of the way into the pass, thereby boxing the soldiers in before making themselves known:

> "[F]rom both sides of that battlemented gorge a fearful rain of fire and lead was poured upon his troops, within a range of from thirty to eighty yards. On either hand the rocks afforded natural and almost unassailable defenses. Every tree concealed an armed warrior, and each warrior boasted his rifle, six-shooter and knife. A better armed host could scarcely be imagined. From behind every species of shelter came the angry and hissing missles, and not a soul to be seen. Quickly, vigorously, and bravely did his men respond, but to what effect? They were expending ammunition to no purpose; their foes were invisible; there was no way to escalade those impregnable natural fortresses; the howitzers were useless, and the men doubtful how to attack the foe. In such strait, Roberts determined to fall back, reform and renew the contest. The orders were given and obeyed with perfect discipline. Reaching the entrance to the pass the troops were reorganized; skirmishers were thrown out over the hills so as to command the road; the howitzers were loaded, and belched forth their shells whenever found necessary. In this manner the troops again marched forward. Water was indispensable for the continuance of life. Unless they could reach the springs they must perish. A march of forty miles under an Arizonian sun, and over wide alkaline plains, with their blinding dust and thirst-provoking effects, had already been effected, and it would be impossible to march back again without serious loss of life, and untold suffering, without taking into account the seeming disgrace of being defeated by seven times their force of Apaches. What would it avail those brave men to know that the Indians were as well armed as they; that they possessed all the advantages; that they outnumbered them seven to one, when the outside and carping world would be so ready to taunt them with defeat, and adduce so many specious reasons why they should have annihilated the savages?

> "Forward, steadily forward, under a continuous and galling fire, did those gallant companies advance until they reached the old station house in the pass, about six hundred yards from the springs. The house was built of stone, and afforded ample shelter; but still they had no water, and eighteen hours, with a march of forty miles, including six hours of sharp fighting, had been passed without a drop. Men and officers were faint, worn-out with fatigue, want of sleep and intense privation and excitement; still Roberts urged them on, and led the way. His person was always the most exposed; his voice ever cheering and encouraging. Immediately commanding the springs were two hills, both high and difficult of ascent. One is to the east, and

the other overlooks them from the south. On these heights the Apaches had built rude but efficient breastworks by piling rocks one upon the other so as to form crenelle holes between the interstices. From these fortifications they kept up a rapid and scathing fire, which could not be returned with effect by musketry from three to four hundred feet below. The howitzers were got into position, but one of them was so badly managed that the gunners wee brought immediately under the fire from the hills without being able to make even a decent response. In a few moments it was overturned by some unaccountable piece of stupidity, and the artillerists driven off by the sharp fire of the Apaches. At that juncture, Sergeant Mitchell with his six associates of my company made a rush to bring off the howitzer and place it in a better position. Upon reaching the guns, they determined not to turn it down the hill, but up, so as to keep their fronts to the fire. While performing this gallant act, they were assailed with a storm of balls, but escaped untouched; after having righted the gun, brought it away, and placed it in a position best calculated to perform effective service. So soon as this feat had been happily accomplished, the exact range was obtained and shell after shell hurled upon the hills, bursting just when they should. The Apaches, wholly unused to such formidable engines, precipitately abandoned their rock works and fled in all directions. It was nearly night. To remain under those death-dealing heights during the night, when campfires would afford the enemy the best kind of advantage, was not true policy, and Captain Roberts ordered each man to take a drink from the precious and hardly-earned springs, and fill his canteen, after which the troops retired within the shelter afforded by the stone station house, the proper guards and pickets being posted."

The soldiers lost two men killed and three wounded. It is unclear how many Apaches were killed, but most estimates range to a dozen or more.

The soldiers knew they couldn't camp in the pass at night without being attacked again, so after drinking at the spring and filling their canteens, they withdrew to rejoin the wagon train. The men were exhausted by a long march and a day of hard fighting, but they had no choice but to retire.

Private John W. Teal lagged behind and the Apaches caught up with him. Some of his comrades were close by but fled and Teal found himself on his own. He related in his diary, "I had mounted & fired my carbine at them, they closed in around me, both mounted & on foot. The chief or commander of the indians was armed with a citizen rifle but was unwilling to fire at me without a rest so, after ralying his warriors, he ran for a rest & I after him but, on looking over my shoulder, I saw the mounted indians to close on my rear for safety, so I turned on them & they scattered like birds. I turned again to tend to the old chief but I was to[o] late, he had got to a bunch of Gaita grass & was lying on his belly on the opposite side of the bunch with his rifle resting on the bunch pointed strait at me, which caused me to drop from the horse on the ground

& the indian shot the horse instead of me. The horse left & I laid low sending a bullet at them whenever I had a chance. We kept firing till it was dark when a lucky shot from me sent the chief30 off in the arms of his indians. I started for the train a few minutes after. I got to the wagons between 10 & 11 oclock P.M. & was verry thirsty, our capt. gave me some whiskey but still I was thirsty. The idea, or thoughts, of fighting for my life against 18 or 20 apacha indians, then travel 8 miles to camp & find no water there would make stronger men than I am thirsty."

The wounded chief was later determined to be Mangas Coloradas himself.

Teal's diary also mentioned the disconcerting sight of Apache signal fires lighting up distant peaks at night, and several skirmishes with Apache who tried to sneak away their horses at night, including one humorous incident where the teamsters hid under sacks of forage while crying "Indians! Indians!" The entry for August 6, 1862 reads in part, "We are travling with Gen. Carlton. Just before we got to cooks springs, for two or three miles, the road is lined with the graves & bones of white people that have been killed by the Indians."

The next day the California column returned to the pass, planning to force their way through. Once again the Apaches opened fire, but this time the soldiers were ready and deployed their artillery, which soon convinced the Apaches to withdraw. The battle led the government to build Fort Bowie in order to protect the water and secure the pass.

With this kind of fighting happening intermittently, pleas from civilian and military authorities alike were finally heard in Washington and more troops were sent to the frontier. Some Confederate prisoners were even offered a way out of dire prison conditions if they took an oath of loyalty to the United States and volunteered for duty on the frontier. Regular troops dubbed them "galvanized Yankees."

It wasn't until after the war, however, with the rush of settlers coming to the region, that anywhere near enough soldiers were sent to do the job. After the Battle of Apache Pass, Cochise and Mangas continued their attacks, despite the fact that Mangas was now about 70 years old. Mangas was captured in 1863, and as the soldiers camped that night with their prize, they tortured him and then allowed him the chance to run so they could claim they had "shot him while trying to escape." He suffered the indignity of having his head cut off, boiled to remove the skin, and sent east for "scientific" examination by the phrenologist Orson Squire Fowler. There could be no worse fate for an Apache; in the Apache afterlife, called Happy Land or Cloud Land, the spirits of the dead existed in the form in which they were buried, so mutilation was considered a fate worse than death. At the same time, the Apache saw such acts as proof that they were fighting barbarians.

Fights against native tribes during the Civil War were not limited to the desert Southwest. The Great Plains also saw its share of fighting thanks to Confederate Brigadier General Albert Pike, commander of the Department of the Indian Territory, modern Oklahoma. He encouraged tribes to raid federal wagon trains and areas occupied by Union forces. The Union, too, tried to get the various tribes on their side, and there was plenty of internecine conflict in the Indian Territory. The Comanche were especially active, raiding both sides as opportunity allowed. With them rode a small, related tribe called the Kiowa-Apache, who were Apache who had moved into the Plains generations earlier and had taken on some characteristics of Plains culture while retaining their Apache identity. Both tribes launched a major raid into Young County, Texas, on 13 October 1864, killing 11 people and capturing 7 women and children and more than 1,000 cattle.

While this was Confederate territory, they were soon raiding the Union areas of Colorado and New Mexico, and famed Indian hunter Kit Carson, who at that time was a Colonel in the Union army, led 335 troops and 75 Indian scouts out to punish the Comanche and Kiowa-Apache. He had perhaps learned a lesson from the California Column's experiences in Apache Pass and brought two artillery pieces along with him. The soldiers marched about 250 miles across almost empty wilderness from Fort Bascom in New Mexico to Adobe Walls in northern Texas. Adobe Walls was an old trading post, abandoned in 1845 but still a notable landmark in the north Texas flatlands.

Kit Carson

The scouts spotted several Comanche and Kiowa-Apache winter camps and in the early hours of November 25, Col. Carson led his men into battle. They were soon spotted and, with surprise lost, Carson ordered his men to charge on the nearest of the camps, the one occupied by the

Kiowa-Apache. Lt. George Pettis, who commanded the small artillery battery and later wrote a pamphlet about the fight, recalled, "We were now in the middle of the rich valley of the Canadian river, which was here about two miles in width, with occasional clumps of cottonwood trees, and covered with tall dry grass, in many places high above our heads when mounted on our horses."

The troops burst out of this cover and descended on the camp. The Kiowa-Apache warriors at first put up a stiff resistance to allow their women and children to escape, and then withdrew to await reinforcements from the other camps. The line of battle reached the old ruins of Adobe Walls, with good visibility on all sides, and here the troops decided to make their stand. "It was now near ten o'clock in the morning, the sky was not obscured by a single cloud, and the sun was shining in all its brightness. Within a hundred yards of the corralled horses in the Adobe Walls, was a small symmetrical conical hill of twenty-five or thirty feet elevation, while in all directions extended a level plain. Carson, McCleave, and a few other officers, occupied the summit, when the battery arrived and took position nearly on the top. Our cavalry was dismounted and deployed as skirmishers in advance, lying in tall grass, and firing an occasional shot at the enemy. Our Indians, mounted and covered with paint and feathers, were charging backwards and forwards and shouting their war cry, and in their front were about two hundred Comanches and Kiowas, equipped as they themselves were, charging in the same manner, with their bodies thrown over the sides of their horses, at a full run, and shooting occasionally under their horses' necks, while the main body of the enemy, numbering twelve or fourteen hundred, with a dozen or more chiefs riding up and down their line haranguing them, seemed to be preparing for a desperate charge on our forces. Surgeon Courtright had prepared a corner of the Adobe Walls for a hospital, and was busy, with his assistants, in attending to the wants of half a dozen or more wounded. Fortunately, the Adobe Walls were high enough to protect all our horses from the enemy's rifles, and afford ample protection to our wounded."

At first the artillery kept the Kiowa-Apache and Comanche at a distance, but as their numbers swelled to a thousand, they grew bolder. Some continued riding back and forth in front of the troops, firing from behind their horses. Others crept up through the grass to snipe at the soldiers. While Carson's men held them off, they were taking casualties (including one unfortunate fellow who was bitten by a snake when lying on the ground) while the Indians' numbers only increased. Carson decided to withdraw, but the Comanche and Kiowa-Apache had no intention of letting the invaders get away.

Pettis wrote that "after we had completed about a mile of our return march, a Comanche rode up to us in a cloud of smoke, when a sudden gust of wind left him completely exposed within twenty feet of the boy who had been bitten by the snake. They both, at the same moment, brought their rifles to their cheeks. The Indian fired a second before the other, and missed his mark, the boy immediately returned the fire, hit his enemy in some vital part, (he instantly fell from off his horse,) and rushed forward to secure his scalp. Some ten or fifteen of the

Comanches who were near, saw their friend fall and rushed forward on their horses to secure the body and bear it away out of our reach, as they had done a great many times during the day. The comrades of the [New] Mexican soldier went to his assistance, kept the enemy at bay until he had finished the scalping operation, and then returned to their places in the skirmish line. This boy took the only scalp that our party secured during the whole day's fight."

The column made it back to the Kiowa-Apache camp and burned it, while Pettis and his guns held off the pursuing Indians. After the destruction was done, Carson led his men on a full retreat. Only the onset of night stopped the deadly pursuit.

At the Battle of Adobe Walls, the U.S. Army lost 2 killed and 21 wounded, with 2 or 3 later dying of their wounds. Carson estimated the Plains Indians lost 60 killed and wounded. Most of these would have been Kiowa-Apache, since they bore the brunt of the initial combat and were in the fight the entire time.

Chapter 5: Escalating Conflict

The end of the Civil War led to a boom in immigration to the Southwest and further encroachment on traditional Apache hunting and gathering grounds. The postwar army was stretched thin and had trouble scouting in the vast deserts and rough mountains, many of which hadn't even been adequately mapped. Civilians, especially newspaper editors, constantly complained that not enough was being done to solve the Indian problem, while at the same time exacerbating that problem by encouraging the hunting down of Indians. Many times, local citizens groups would find an Apache rancheria and burn it to cinders, killing anyone they could catch.

Apache retribution was equally heartless. On 26 May 1870, a wagon train of merchandise left Tucson heading for Camp Grant, 55 miles to the northeast. The wagon train was owned and led by High Kennedy and Newton Israel and included several women and children. They never made it. A group of some 50 or 60 Apaches descended on the wagons and killed all the men, carrying off the women and children. One of the officers from Camp Grant, Captain John Bourke, described the scene when he got there: "There were hot embers of the new wagons, the scattered fragments of broken boxes, barrels, one or two broken rifles, torn and burned clothing. There lay all that was mortal of poor Israel, stripped of clothing, a small piece cut from the crown of the head, but thrown back upon the corpse—the Apaches do not care much for scalping—his heart cut out, but also thrown back near the corpse, which had been dragged to the fire of the burning wagons and partly consumed; a lance wound in the back one or two arrow wounds, a severe contusion under the left eye, where he had been hit perhaps with the stock of a rifle or carbine, and the death wound from ear to ear, through which the brain had oozed. The face was as calm and resolute in death as Israel had been in life."

The cavalry expedition that went after the marauders was led by the experienced Indian fighter

Lt. Howard Cushing, whose command was distinguished by bringing two scouts intimately familiar with the Apache. One, Manuel Duran, was actually a friendly Apache, while the other, Joe Felmer was married to one. Felmer is recorded to have given the soldiers this nugget of frontier wisdom: "When you see Apache 'sign', be *keerful*; 'n' when you don' see nary sign, be *more* keerful."

The trackers' work was made easier by a trail of empty patent medicine bottles. The Apaches had found these opium and alcohol concoctions and had enjoyed them as much the many whites who were addicted to them in the 19th century. The trail soon became harder to follow as the raiders sobered up and doubled back over their path, frequently also crossing rocky ground in order to hide their passing. Like with many later expeditions that relied on Apache trackers, the whites commented that the trails these men followed were invisible to all but the Apache.

The trail passed Camp Grant by only a few miles and led into the Pinal Mountains and to a valley, where the soldiers finally spotted the raiders' dust cloud in the distance. Waiting until nightfall, Lt. Cushing led his men to the Apache camp and surrounded it. The Apaches must have thought they were safe because they hadn't posted sentries, a fatal mistake. The soldiers quietly surrounded the camp and were about to strike when they were spotted. They then loosed a hail of gunfire into the wikiups. The official report states that the soldiers killed 30 Apaches, some of them children caught in the crossfire, and captured many more, with no losses to themselves.

Lt. Cushing then went on an extended campaign in 1871 to track down Cochise, but he died in an ambush when Apaches lured him and his vanguard into a canyon and shot at them from three sides.

Attacks like these led to persistent complaints by the Arizona Territorial government. In 1871 it published Memorial and Affidavits Showing Outrages Perpetrated by the Apache Indians in order to list some of the attacks made by the Apache in the previous two years and bring awareness to the plight of the settlers. While the document is probably guilty of exaggeration in order to further its political goals, it does show some interesting trends.

First, it noted that the Apache often attacked the same ranches over and over again. Louis Quesse, who lived near Tubac, reported that between January 1869 and October 1870, he lost in nine separate attacks 11 horses, 88 cattle, and two mules, plus three workers injured. Frederick Marsh lost from his ranch near Tucson 40 head of cattle and four horses in six different incidents in 1870 alone.

There are also frequent mentions of attacks on mail deliveries. This may seem odd until it is remembered that in the days before extensive banking and the use of checks, cash was regularly sent through the mail, and the booklet recounts numerous cases of Apaches buying liquor, guns, and ammunition with greenbacks.

Harder to explain was the destruction of crops. This could be of no practical purpose for the Apache and went against their usual methods and reasons for raiding. It may have been the product of some optimistic individuals who thought they could drive the settlers out of the region altogether.

An even more bizarre incident was the theft of some tents from right behind the officers' quarters at Camp Crittenden! Numerous reports complained about the roads not being safe for anything but large, well-armed groups, and that Apache residing on reservations would often slip away to raid.

One incident that didn't make it into the Arizona government's list of outrages was the worst outrage of the period. In late 1870, a group of Arivaipa Apache had requested to settle near Camp Grant. They said they were tired of running from the cavalry and had no place to stay. The newly arrived commander, Lt. Royal Whitman, eagerly agreed, and provided supplies to the Apache as well as finding them jobs on the local ranches. It was the first impromptu attempt by the Americans at making a reservation for the Apache.

At first all went well, but some Anglos and Mexicans in nearby Tucson were nervous at having a several hundred Apache so close by. In addition, many traders were making good profits by selling to the soldiers and if the Apache problem were solved, they stood to lose their business. There was much grumbling about Whitman's experiment. Then, on 10 May 1871, a baggage train was attacked not far from Tucson and two men were killed. Ten days later a rancher was killed and a Mexican woman kidnapped not far from the city.

Blame immediately fell on the Arivaipa, although Whitman was convinced they were innocent. The newspapers railed against Whitman and the Arivaipa, and when there were further attacks, the Anglos and Mexicans in Tucson met secretly to form an armed party to punish them. Hearing the Arivaipa men were away at a dance, the vigilantes slipped out of town in small groups so as not to attract attention, met up with some Papago tribesmen who wanted to be in on the fun, and on 30 April, they descended on the almost undefended settlement. By the time Whitman got word of the attack and rode with his men to the rescue, it was all over. The camp had been torched and 118 Apache killed, all but eight of them women and children. The raiders had also taken 28 children to sell into slavery. Only seven of the Apache were able to escape.

One who did was Mbalsesla, also known as Sherman Curley, who was a young man at the time. Recalling the incident in the 1930s, he had this to say:

> "There was a big ridge above their camps, and one on the other side too. During the night a big bunch of Mexicans and Papagos had got up on these ridges, and surrounded the camp completely. The Mexicans and Papagos. . .fired on them while they were still dancing. They killed a lot of people this way. They all scattered. The scouts and soldiers down at Camp Grant didn't know what was going on. I ran into

an arroyo. I had my bow and arrows, and I pointed at them as if I was going to shoot. This scared some Mexicans and Papagos back, who were after me. I ran on, trying to get away, but four of them followed me, but they did not kill me or hit me. In those days we Apaches could run fast, but we cannot do this now. I ran in behind some rocks, below an overhanging bluff finally, and hid there. They shot at me, but could not hit me those four enemies. They four were afraid to come close. I shot arrows at them. Finally they ran away, and left me. I ran on up the side of the mountain, to the top, and stayed there. Some others who had gotten away were on top of this mountain also. . .The sun was getting really low now. We stayed on top of this mountain all night. The next day one man went back to place where we had been dancing. He found lots of dead Apaches there.

"Some of the women and girls who had long, nice hair, they had cut a round place right out of the scalp, leaving the hair on, and taken it away with them. I don't know why they did this. This man came back, and told about it."

There was a show trial in Tucson, but none of the culprits were ever punished. The message was clear: killing Apaches was not a crime.

Chapter 6: General Crook and the Beginning of the End

The controversy over the Camp Grant Massacre made national news, and while the perpetrators were never brought to justice, the federal government saw a need for a change. In May 1871, the government replaced General Stoneman, the commander of the Department of Arizona, with a new man, General George Crook, in the hope that he could finally bring peace and order to the region. Crook turned out to be the man for the job.

General Crook

Crook came to the Arizona with a distinguished military career fighting Indians and Confederates. He was, by all accounts, sober, humble, and willing to listen to those who knew the local area better than he. While he was fully prepared to defeat the Apache militarily, he was also sympathetic to the needs of those who wanted peace.

Once he was in Tucson, he wasted no time. He called in officers from all parts of the Arizona Territory and grilled them about conditions on the ground. Then he set out to hunt down Cochise and other hostile Apaches. He hired Mexican scouts for their knowledge of the land and their willingness to fight, but soon became dissatisfied with them. They often ignored commands from lower-grade officers and failed to discriminate between friendly and hostile Apaches. Having suffered from years of Apache depredations, the Mexicans wanted to eliminate all Apaches. Revenge was more important than discipline.

Then Crook hit on the idea of using Indian scouts. Whether or not he knew of the Spanish experiments of the previous century is unclear, but to his astute mind the advantages were obvious; they knew the land better than anyone, were expert trackers, spoke the language, and could tell friend from foe. At first he hired Pima and Navajo. While they proved better than the Mexicans, local commanders complained that they were reluctant to fight. Some even accused the scouts of leading the U.S. Cavalry away from the Apache in order to avoid contact.

Finally Crook decided to take a gamble by hiring Apaches to hunt Apaches. While this seemed a bad idea to some, Crook understood Apache culture better than any other high-ranking officer in the West. It is common practice to look upon "inferior" or "native" cultures as a monolithic people, thinking in lockstep with one another, but Crook saw beyond that and understood that Apaches were highly individualistic, their scattered bands having little formal leadership and looking out for their own interests. It was easy to find settled Apaches eager to take regular pay to fight fellow Apaches.

Apache scouts signed on for a six-month service, which was later extended. An Apache who signed up for less than six months had to supply his own horse and equipment, and at first, they were issued with a Civil War surplus uniforms and weapons. In battle they tended to discard the uniform and fight Apache fashion, wearing only the traditional loincloth and moccasin boots, plus a red bandanna so that their white comrades wouldn't shoot them by mistake.

Success was instantaneous. Crook tirelessly hunted down hostile bands and the Apache scouts proved expert at leading him to them. There were problems, however. While Apache scouts were relatively free of the strict discipline regular soldiers endured, they were still placed in an ordered regime alien to them. Disagreements and misunderstandings often arose over their terms of stay. In a traditional Apache raiding party, an individual could leave at any time. This, of course, was not allowed in the U.S. Cavalry.

Another problem was that of personal vendettas. Some Apaches signed up as scouts to even scores with enemies. If sent against groups with whom they had sympathy, they sometimes led the cavalry astray or warned their friends of the cavalry's intentions.

There was also the risk of social alienation. Many Apache saw these scouts as traitors. For example, the Chiricahua scout Chato, or Flat Nose, who was well-respected by cavalry officers and even headed the delegation to Washington to discuss the removal of Apaches to the East in 1886, had a bad reputation among many Apaches. He was considered a brute and a bully, but his unpardonable sin was aligning himself with the U.S. Cavalry under false circumstances. He had joined in 1883 after a failed bid to become an Apache war leader. Chato was soon first sergeant of Company B, Apache Scouts under the command of 2nd Lt. Britton Davis, despite there being many more experienced scouts in the unit. The Apaches claimed he had Mickey Free, another scout and "coyote" (renegade), translate falsely in order to make Chato look good and to hurt the reputation of respected leaders such as Geronimo and Chihuahua. Mickey Free told Davis that the two leaders were trying to kill him.

Despite these troubles, hiring Apaches as scouts proved to be a resounding success, and many soldiers admitted they could have never defeated the Apaches without them. Hostile Apaches agreed. James Kaywaykla, who rode with Victorio, later said that "it was the scouts whom the Apaches dreaded, for only they knew the trails and the hiding places. And only they could traverse the country rapidly enough to be a menace."

In addition to military changes, there were also civilian changes. Despite the disaster at Camp Grant, settling tribes on reservations was gaining favor in political circles. In 1872, the Camp Grant settlement was moved north to the Gila River, well away from Tucson, and renamed the San Carlos Reservation. The San Carlos and White Mountain reservations were established that same year.

Crook was pleased with developments but remained convinced that those Apache that had not already settled onto reservations would have to be forced to do so. The year 1872 had seen many raids by "wild" Apache, and parts of the Arizona Territory were all but uninhabitable for whites and Mexicans. Thus, he launched an offensive in November 1872, the goal of which was to eradicate the defeat the numerous bands of hostile Apaches and force them onto reservations once and for all. He sent out several columns into the areas of eastern Arizona where resistance was at its height, with the goal of attacking the rancherias and driving the Apaches into the snow-capped mountains, where privation would eventually force them to submit to government authority. Each column was well supplied with Apache scouts as well as mule trains and packers. This latter element of the campaign was an innovation of Crook's. Earlier campaigns had all too often relied on cumbersome supply wagons that were slow on good ground and useless in the mountains. Some commanders had tried mules before, but Crook hired the best packers in the territory to ensure that the operation ran efficiently.

His officers were ordered to accept surrender if offered, and prisoners should be fairly treated. Those who didn't surrender would be tenaciously pursued. Rancherias and supplies would be burned to deny the renegades any comfort.

From November through March the columns crisscrossed the countryside, fighting numerous skirmishes with the Apache and capturing a growing tally of prisoners. Those Apaches who managed to avoid capture were run to exhaustion. They found few places to run and hide, since the Apache scouts knew all of their tricks and shelters. They struck at the heart of Apacheria, and the hostile bands' morale suffered.

The scouts generally roved 12-24 hours ahead of the main column, with instructions to locate the hostile Apache and report back to the soldiers. Being Apache, however, they were eager for battle and often all the fighting was done by the time the main force of soldiers arrived. Doubts about the scouts' willingness and ability to fight vanished, at least among the soldiers.

Captain John Bourke wrote of them, "The longer we knew the Apache scouts, the better we liked them. They were wilder and more suspicious than the Pimas and Maricopas, but far more reliable, and endowed with a greater amount of courage and daring. I have never known an officer whose experience entitled his opinion to the slightest consideration, who did not believe as I do on this subject."

It was a grueling campaign with little rest for either side. Bourke, who marched in Major William Brown's column, recorded that in 142 days they had killed 500 Apache and traveled 1,200 miles. In the first week of April 1873, representatives from several hostile bands appeared at Camp Verde asking for peace. Large-scale resistance was over, but the fighting would continue for a further 13 years. A few diehards like Victorio and Geronimo still defied the Americans, and conditions on the reservation proved unacceptable to some warriors, who fled to rejoin the fighting and live the way they always had.

When one considers the conditions on the various Apache reservations, it's a wonder that more didn't flee. Rations were often insufficient and of poor quality, when they were distributed at all, and corrupt and abuses on the part of the Indian Agency were rife. The Apaches were put on poor land and not allowed to hunt as they were accustomed. Often hostile bands would be placed side by side with no understanding of the trouble this might cause. Faced with hunger, disease, danger, and the humiliation of capture, some Apaches preferred to live free and die fighting.

Matters would change for the better in August 1874, when John Clum arrived to take over management of the San Carlos Reservation. Only 23 years old, he arrived with little experience but a keen eye for cultural differences and little innate prejudice against Native Americans. He quickly grew to know and respect the Apache, who in turn grew to love him. He saw that outbreaks were the result of corruption and miserable conditions and worked hard to eliminate both. He gave the Apaches paid jobs building facilities for the reservation and made sure everyone got their fair share of rations.

More controversially, he established an Indian court, with himself as chief justice, as well as an Indian police force. These two measures got a great amount of criticism from the local and national press, but he persevered. The Apache police program was soon expanded and did a good job stamping out illegal liquor and chasing down runaways. A major test came when Clum ordered the warrior Desalin to stop beating his two wives. Desalin, deeply insulted at this affront to his manhood, tried to kill him. Clum was saved by an Apache policeman named Tauelclyee, who happened to be Desalin's brother.

The Apache police proved so effective, Clum used them as a sort of miniature army to round up other bands and concentrate them at the San Carlos. In this he was only moderately successful, as he soon found that hunting hostile Apache in the wilderness was much more difficult than giving friendly Apaches a square deal on the reservation. He soon had nearly all the Western Apache under his protection.

James Kaywaykla, who was a boy at the time, recalled that the Apaches admired Clum. "As agents went, John Clum was one of the best. The Apaches conceded that; but they knew also that he was responsible for the Chiricahua's reservation being taken from them, and that he caused the removal of Apaches from Cochise's reservation to San Carlos so that they would be under his jurisdiction. And they knew, too, that his motive for attempting to bring all Apaches under his rule was an increase in salary; they knew, too, that he did not get it. They respected the arrogant young man in spite of that, for he was courageous and honest. They believed him to be unique in that respect, having dealt with many of the breed. They liked his using Indian police and Indian judges. At that time both press and pulpit were debating the question of whether or not Indians possessed souls and it was commendable to have a man who realized that our standards differed from his people. Our standards are, at that, not so vastly different from those of the White Eyes except for the fact we set great store by promises and rigidly enforced chastity."

The main holdout was Victorio and the Warm Springs band of the Chihenne Apache, who roved southern New Mexico, raiding on both sides of the border. Clum tracked him down in 1877 and convinced his band to come to San Carlos. They were unhappy there, being packed in with other bands with whom they didn't get along, and when Clum resigned in July over political wrangling between the Indian Service and the Army, matters grew worse. Once again supplies fell short, being skimmed off by corrupt officials. The Apache were supposed to farm, but were given few tools or seeds, little training, and in any case the land was harsh desert.

With Clum gone, there was no one to see to the Apaches' interests at San Carlos and in September a large group of Chihennes and Chiricahuas under Victorio and Loco broke out and fled east, looting as they went and fighting a running battle with the U.S. Cavalry. They eventually gave themselves up and were returned to San Carlos, but broke out again in August 1879. Kaywaykla and his family went with them. "It was a hard life, but we liked it better than the hopeless stagnation of the reservation. . .Again we had hope for freedom. Hardships imposed on people are much more onerous than those they voluntarily assume," he recalled.

Leading about 200 warriors and many women and children, Victorio headed for Ojo Caliente, where they had lived and prospered before being sent to the reservation. The clashed with a small patrol of Buffalo Soldiers, killing five and then setting out to raid the local settlers, killing several of them. Soon, large columns of U.S. Cavalry were scouring the countryside for the runaways.

On September 18 at Las Animas Canyon, Victorio fought a brilliant battle against pursuing cavalry that amply demonstrated the Apache's genius for using the terrain to their advantage.

The band was being followed by two companies of Buffalo soldiers in the Black Mountains of New Mexico. The Apaches deliberately left a trail through a river gorge, then circled back and hid in the high ground to both sides. The troops, led by four Navajo guides, entered the canyon. The Navajo sensed a trap but the officer in charge, Captain Byron Dawson, urged his men forward.

The first they knew of the Apaches was a fusillade of bullets coming in from seemingly all directions. There was little cover, and the men had to hide behind their horses, who were soon falling at an alarming rate. By noon, the men were running low on ammunition when they were reinforced by two more companies of troops and some volunteers from a nearby mining camp. This force was similarly pinned down and the battle only ended with the coming of night.

While losses were fairly low—two scouts, one civilian, and three cavalrymen killed—the column had lost many of their mounts and were forced to leave much of their supplies behind. Victorio grabbed the much-needed food and blankets and hurried away.

Victorio continued to run the U.S. Cavalry ragged, eluding several columns in Arizona and New Mexico and fighting several skirmishes in which he always came out the victor, or at least not the loser. Kaywaykla remembered one amusing incident while on the march. Nana, one of Victorio's assistants, had told the thirsty Apaches not to drink from a certain stream, and they soon found out why when they stopped to fight the pursuing soldiers. "The cavalry had drunk the water Nana had forbidden us to touch, and so had their horses. Both had become ill from a laxative effect, and were weakened until they could hardly travel. We had not poisoned that spring; the illness was caused by a natural mineral that this time operated in our favor. The troops were easily beaten back."

All this fighting was wearing down his band, however. While the soldiers had an inexhaustible supply of ammunition and reinforcements, every bullet the Apaches fired had to be replaced with another raid, and the dead warriors could never be replaced. Eventually Victorio led the remnants of his band into Mexico, where he was cornered on 14 October 1880. He and most of his band were gunned down. This last fight was mostly one-sided. Victorio's men were all but out of ammunition. Only a few warriors managed to break away to fight another day.

The death of Victorio was the beginning of the end for Apache resistance. Nana, who had been with Victorio when he was killed in Mexico, escaped and continued to fight. On an epic raid in 1881, the Warm Springs Apache leader, who was about 70 years of age, led a few dozen warriors over a thousand miles in six weeks, fighting numerous skirmishes with the U.S. Cavalry and killing up to 50 people. Loco was another of the holdouts, alternating between a settled life at San Carlos and wide-ranging raids across the Southwest.

Both of these raiders set off panics in the territories, but in general life was becoming more peaceful. Most of the Apaches had resigned themselves to reservation life and there were few breakouts.

It must have seemed to the Americans and Mexicans that their Apache troubles were over, but there was one more fighter who would refuse to submit. His name would become synonymous with Native American resistance, and although he was not the greatest or even most popular leader among his people, his is the name that is still remembered in modern times.

Chapter 7: The Geronimo Campaign

"I have killed many Mexicans; I do not know how many, for frequently I did not count them. Some of them were not worth counting. It has been a long time since then, but still I have no love for the Mexicans. With me they were always treacherous and malicious." - Geronimo

Sometime in the 1820s (probably June 1829), an Apache boy named Goyahkla was born near the headwaters of the Gila River in No-doyohn Canyon, Arizona. His people called themselves Bedonkohe and were closely related to the Chiricahuas, often submitting to their chiefs.

While Native Americans were often victims in the Southwest, members of the warrior societies were also guilty of killing and robbing settlers or traders. Chiricahua bands living in this border region had long experienced a tense relationship with the Mexicans, whom they viewed as invaders. Apache raids had led to the Mexican government offering bounties on Apache scalps, including children's scalps, but the Apache groups continued the raids anyway. By the time he was 17, Goyahkla had led 4 successful raids himself.

The events that would transform the young Goyahkla into the man known today as Geronimo took place in 1851 outside the northern Mexican town of Janos, which the Natives called Kas-ki-yeh. Goyahkla's narrative says that the entire Bedonkohe band was traveling to the Mexican town of Casa Grande but had stopped at Kas-ki-yeh (Janos) for several days, which they regarded as peaceful and safe. Each day, the men of the band left a small guard protecting the camp, women, children, ponies, arms, and supplies and walked into the town to trade with the town folk. Upon returning to their encampment one day, the men found their people massacred, their ponies captured, their arms secured, and their supplies destroyed by marauding Mexican cavalry troops under Colonel José María Carrasco. The men scattered and each made his way alone to the rendezvous place designated in case of trouble. Survivors of the massacre and the men gradually made their ways to the rendezvous.

After the survivors had reached the rendezvous and a count was conducted, Goyahkla found that his mother, his wife Alope, and his three young children were not among them. He would describe the massacre in his autobiography:

"Late one afternoon when returning from town we were met by a few women and children who told us that Mexican troops from some other town had attacked our camp, killed all the warriors of the guard, captured all our ponies, secured our arms, destroyed our supplies, and killed many of our women and children. Quickly we separated, concealing ourselves as best we could until nightfall, when we assembled at our appointed place of rendezvous—a thicket by the river. Silently we stole in one by one: sentinels were placed, and, when all were counted, I found that my aged mother, my young wife, and my three small children were among the slain. There were no lights in camp, so without being noticed I silently turned away and stood by the river. How long I stood there I do not know, but when I saw the warriors arranging for a council I took my place."

By 1868, Goyahkla had earned the name Geronimo through his exploits against the Mexican people, but it's still unclear how the name Geronimo came about, and historians still debate it. What is known is that during one fight against the Mexicans, Geronimo ignored a deadly hail of bullets and attacked Mexican soldiers with a knife. Some historians believe that the name came about because the soldiers he was attacking cried out to St. Jerome with the word "Jeronimo". Other historians believe Mexican soldiers simply mispronounced the name Goyahkla when referring to him.

Following the death of Cochise in 1874, Geronimo rose to a position of leadership among the Chiricahua Apache, and a few years later, he would earn recognition as one of the most skilled guerrilla fighters in American history. Though Geronimo neglects to mention it in his autobiography, he was part of a group of Chiricahuas from several different bands who spent much of 1882 raiding in Chihuahua and the southwestern United States. In 1883, Geronimo and the other Chiricahuas returned to Mexico and spent over a year in the mountains, likely raiding and stealing. Again the Chiricahuas operated like a guerilla army without the political end goal, living off of the land and the populace. As was their practice, they avoided direct conflict with Mexican troops but engaged them in numerous small actions. In response to an increased Mexican military presence in the mountains, the Chiricahuas returned to Arizona in 1884, hoping to recruit additional warriors to the cause of successful raiding in the mountains of northern Mexico. Unfortunately for the Chiricahuas, they had a conflict of some kind with U.S. troops and lost fifteen warriors. At least, that is the way Geronimo describes the actions of the Chiricahua bands after returning to Arizona. Other sources say the Bedonkohe and members of other Chiricahua bands surrendered and were taken to the San Carlos Indian Reservation.

Geronimo's 1885 escape from the San Carlos Indian Reservation marked the start of his final campaign, and ten months after leaving the reservation, Geronimo and his followers would surrender to U.S. troops in Mexico. Geronimo entered this surrender probably because he trusted the man accepting his surrender, General George R. Crook, a veteran of Phil Sheridan's Shenandoah Valley Campaign in 1864. The Apache had nicknamed Crook "Nantan Lupan," meaning Grey Wolf, and the General had earned a reputation for honesty among the Plains tribes while he served as the commander of the District of the Platte. However, as the small group of

Native Americans marched north toward the border escorted by U.S. troops, Geronimo and a group of about 35 other Chiricahuas slipped away, fearing they'd be murdered. Two weeks later, there were reports that Geronimo and his group had massacred a family near Silver City, and that one girl was hanged from a meat hook jammed under the base of her skull. Whether the story was true or not, it certainly created a great deal of apprehension in the region.

General Crook, who had assumed command of the Arizona Territory in 1882, immediately resigned his command. Ten days later, one of the most hardened American veterans of the Indian Wars, General Nelson A. Miles, arrived in the territory, assumed command, and proceeded to change the tactics being used to find and capture Geronimo. Crook's replacement had already enjoyed success in pursuing and capturing Native American leaders and their followers, having force-marched across Montana with his troops in 1877 to capture Chief Joseph of the Nez Perce tribe. In that campaign, the Nez Perce led U.S. troops on a chase that covered over 1,000 miles.

Nelson Miles

Miles drastically diminished the role played by Native American troops – the Apache Scouts – in the effort to find and capture Geronimo, and he quickly deployed some 5,500 U.S. troops in new roles. Some troops were assigned to active patrolling and conducting search and destroy operations in Mexico searching for the Chiricahuas. Additionally, Miles assigned troops to guard all known water holes in the arid region. Despite this massive effort, which had U.S. troops in pursuit of Geronimo traveling over 1,500 miles, Miles was no closer to finding and capturing the small Chiricahua band three months later. At this point Miles had to reassess his strategy, and he decided to send an officer with a small party into Mexico to find Geronimo and negotiate a surrender. The new strategy required General Miles to choose an officer from among those remaining from General Crook's command, because none of his men were familiar with the Chiricahua or spoke their language.

Miles settled on Lieutenant Charles B. Gatewood. A graduate of the United States Military Academy at West Point in 1877, Charles Gatewood had been assigned to the 6th Cavalry Regiment stationed at Fort Wingate, New Mexico. After a year of service at Fort Wingate, the young officer was assigned to command companies of Apache and Navajo scouts in Apache country throughout the southwest. Applying an unusually modern approach and style while serving as the leader of Native American scout companies, Gatewood believed that his best chance for success with the Apache and Navajo troops would come by understanding their culture and attitudes and gaining their acceptance.

The Chiricahua called Gatewood "Baychendaysen" ("Long Nose")

In an effort to achieve these goals, Gatewood met with his troops daily, dismissed ideas of his own racial superiority, and avoided talking down to his Native American soldiers. Lieutenant Gatewood appeared to have a promising Army career ahead of him, but in 1884, he arrested a territorial judge for fraud committed against his Native American wards. General Crook asked

Gatewood to drop the charges against the Judge but the Lieutenant refused, and the ensuing litigation eventually made it impossible for Crook and Gatewood to work together.

Lieutenant Gatewood was transferred and assigned to command a company of Navajo scouts. By the time Gatewood was assigned to the pursuit of Geronimo, he had nine years of service in the Southwest and had spent the three years prior to his appointment in charge of the Fort Apache agency. The officer had spent nearly 10 years in the field with Apaches – fighting with and against them – and was intimately familiar with their values and traditions. Most importantly, Gatewood was well known to Geronimo and knew every member of the Bedonkohe warrior's band, and the Chiricahua had nicknamed him Baychendaysen, which roughly translates to "Long Nose." The presence and service of Charles Gatewood was very likely the only reason the effort to convince Geronimo and his companions to surrender was ultimately successful, and Gatewood's revolutionary attitude towards both his enemy and his own troops probably guaranteed both his survival and the success of his mission.

General Miles' plan involved sending two Chiricahua Apaches whom the U.S. commander considered "friendly," Kayitah and Martine, to carry a message to Geronimo. The two men would be accompanied on the mission by Lieutenant Gatewood and were chosen because both were related to members of Geronimo's party. Gatewood would carry written orders from General Miles authorizing him to requisition any assistance he might need to complete his mission from U.S. military units operating in the field, and the General forbade Gatewood from approaching the Chiricahuas without an escort of at least 25 troops. Gatewood was allowed to pick other team members and recruited interpreter George Wratten and packer Frank Huston to accompany him into Mexico.

After outfitting at Fort Bowie in the Arizona Territory, the party departed for Mexico, all members riding mules. At a U.S. military camp near the Mexican border, Gatewood had planned to acquire the 25 soldiers Miles expected him to deploy as he approached Geronimo and his band, but the camp was woefully undermanned and its commander was one of Gatewood's instructors at West Point, who quaked when presented with Miles' written orders. It was clear to Gatewood that he could not strip the outpost of its manpower, so he chose not to take an escort in Mexico with him and relied on gaining assistance from one of the U.S. columns operating south of the border. Just before Gatewood crossed into Mexico, Tex Whaley, a courier, joined the party. The date was July 19, 1886.

At the time, Mexico and the United States had an agreement that allowed U.S. troops to cross into Mexico and conduct operations there in pursuit of hostile Native Americans. Soon after crossing the border, an escort commanded by Captain James Parker, joined the Gatewood party. Parker's command consisted of a troop of cavalry from the 4th Cavalry Regiment and infantry detachments from the 8th and 10th Infantry Regiments; the Captain's entire command consisted of less than 40 troops. Once again, Gatewood's attempt to requisition a detachment of 25 troops to escort him close to Geronimo and his band was thwarted, in large part by Gatewood's consideration of the state and mission of the unit he encountered. Parker also had orders to follow Geronimo's trail, but as he explained to Gatewood, "The trail is all a myth. I haven't seen any trail since three weeks ago when it was washed out by the rains."

Sometime around the middle of August, as Lawton and his command wandered northward, word came that Geronimo and his band were in the vicinity of Fronteras, which meant about 70 miles of Sonoran desert separated Gatewood from his target. Gatewood immediately began preparing to depart for Fronteras and received a six-man escort from Lawton that joined the two Chiricahuas (Martine and Kayitah), the interpreter (Wratten), and several packers as they departed at 2:00 a.m. the following morning. The party marched and rode the bulk of the distance in one day, arriving at Cuchuta late on the same night. On or about August 20, Gatewood and his party covered the remaining fifteen miles to Fronteras.

Upon arrival in the Mexican town, Gatewood learned that several Chiricahua women had approached the Mexican officials with an offer of surrender and that U.S. Lieutenant W.E. Wilder had spoken with them about surrendering. The women had departed, heading east and leading ponies laden with food and mescal. Lieutenant Gatewood presented himself to the Prefect of the District of Arizpe, Jesus Aguirre and relayed the nature of his mission to district official (Fronteras fell under the jurisdiction of the District of Arizpe). Prefecto Aguirre was skeptical of Gatewood's mission, and the meeting between the two men was unproductive. Also, the Prefecto had raised a force of some 200 Mexicans and meant to make good on his threat to kill Geronimo and those with him.

Leaving Fronteras, Gatewood led his party south and made camp with a group of U.S. soldiers bivouacked there. During the night, Aguirre entered the camp and warned the U.S. troops not to follow the Chiricahua women because doing so would spoil plans he had set into motion. He told Gatewood and the other officers that he intended to once again use the old trick of getting the Apaches drunk and then murdering the entire group. While it's unclear who commanded the troops camped south of Fronteras, it seems to have been Lieutenant Wilder, because in his account Gatewood states that Lieutenant Wilder detached troops to accompany him when he again departed in pursuit of Geronimo.

For two days, Gatewood and his party did not attempt to contact Geronimo. The next morning, the party picked up the trail of the Chiricahua women and began tracking them towards Geronimo's hideout. Gatewood followed the trails for three days and sent a courier to Lawton to inform him of his progress. The trail led the Gatewood party through a canyon and on to the Bavispe River. Once the party arrived in the river valley, it became clear by the signs that the Chiricahua band was nearby. Choosing a nearby cane break that offered a good view of the surrounding country, Gatewood set up camp around midday, on or about August 24, 1886. Another courier was sent to Lawton, apprising him of the situation, and Kyitah and Martine were dispatched to find Geronimo and the Chiricahuas. Gatewood was tiring of his assignment as a peace envoy and commented wryly in his account that the white flag of peace does not render a man bulletproof. Ha also noted that he later learned that Geronimo had been observing his small party the whole time they were approaching, wondering what kind of fool was trailing him.

Following Wood's orders, Gatewood, Tom Horn, Jesus Maria Yestes, and six or eight of Wilder's troopers departed around dusk, heading eastward. Horn was serving as the Chief of Scouts for one of Miles's column's operating inside Mexico. By heading east, as though following Captain Lawton's column, Gatewood hoped to deceive Aguirre and frustrate his plans to massacre the Chiricahuas. The party traveled about six miles before darkness fell, allowing Gatewood to circle back to the north and head back towards Fronteras.

The next morning, the party picked up the trail of the Chiricahua women and began tracking them towards Geronimo's hideout. Gatewood followed the trails for three days and sent a courier to Lawton to inform him of his progress. The trail led the Gatewood party through a canyon and on to the Bavispe River. Once the party arrived in the river valley, it became clear by the signs that the Chiricahua band was nearby. Choosing a nearby cane break that offered a good view of the surrounding country, Gatewood set up camp around midday, on or about August 24, 1886. Another courier was sent to Lawton, apprising him of the situation, and Kyitah and Martine were dispatched to find Geronimo and the Chiricahuas. Gatewood was tiring of his assignment as a peace envoy and commented wryly in his account that the white flag of peace does not render a man bulletproof. Ha also noted that he later learned that Geronimo had been observing his small party the whole time they were approaching, wondering what kind of fool was trailing him.

In the evening of the day they established the camp, Lieutenant R.A. Brown and a force of about 30 Native American scouts arrived in camp and reported that Lawton's command was nearby. Shortly after the arrival of Brown and his scouts, Martine returned to the camp and reported that he and Kayitah had delivered General Miles's message to Geronimo and that Kayitah had remained in the Chiricahua camp. Martine also reported that Geronimo's camp was located on very rocky high ground, on a bend in the Bavispe River, and that Geronimo and Naiche – the ancestral Chiricahua chief – were willing to discuss their surrender, but only with Gatewood. The approach of darkness made visiting Geronimo impossible that evening, so the group camped for the night in the cane break.

The following morning, Gatewood packed the fifteen pounds of tobacco and cigarette rolling papers he had requested in anticipation of the meeting with the Chiricahua and which arrived from Lawton overnight. At dawn, Gatewood's party set out toward Geronimo's hiding place, escorted by Brown and his 30 Native American scouts. As they approached the mountain where the Chiricahuas were hiding, the force encountered an unarmed Chiricahua, attempting to deliver the same message that Martine had carried to the U.S. soldiers the night before. Shortly afterwards, three armed warriors appeared and stated that Geronimo would meet with Gatewood at a bend in the river, where there was wood, water, grass, and shade, but the wary Chiricahua would only attend the meeting if Brown and his scouts retreated to the cane break where the force had bivouacked the night before.

Gatewood acquiesced and sent Brown and his troops back to the cane break and told him that any additional troops that might join them should stay there as well. The reduced party, now down to Gatewood, Martine, Wratten, Yestes, Horn, possibly one soldier, and the four Chiricahuas, continued on to Geronimo's designated meeting place. After they had advanced for some time, Chiricahuas suddenly appeared on the mountain above them. They then disappeared and reappeared at the mountain's base emerging from a number of different directions and numbering about 35, of whom 20 or so were warriors. Geronimo was not among them.

Gatewood greeted all the Chiricahuas and removed his arms. The Chiricahuas asked for alcohol and tobacco. Tobacco and cigarette papers were passed out, and Gatewood explained that he had no alcohol. Everyone rolled cigarettes and began smoking. Geronimo appeared, and after putting down his Winchester he approached Gatewood, shaking hands with him and commenting on the Lieutenant's sickly appearance. The two sat close together, too close for Gatewood's comfort, and talked. Geronimo said that he and his people were there to hear General Miles' offer regarding their surrender. In short order, Gatewood relayed the General's message: Geronimo was to surrender unconditionally and join the remainder of his people in Florida to await the final disposition of his case by the President of the United States. Geronimo had to accept these terms or fight to the bitter end.

Geronimo attempted to negotiate with Gatewood, but the Lieutenant said he was only ordered to deliver the General's message and had no authority to negotiate terms. The Chiricahuas retreated a bit and discussed the matter among themselves, apart from the soldiers. It being midday, the participants ate lunch and afterwards resumed their discussions. Geronimo then entered into a long listing of the wrongs suffered by his people at the hands of whites and concluded by saying that expecting the Chiricahuas to give up everything to a bunch of intruders was too much. They were willing to give up all of their former territory except the reservation, demanding that Gatewood allow them to return to the reservation or fight. Gatewood repeated his inability to negotiate terms, saying he couldn't take them to the reservation and he couldn't fight with them.

It was decided that the formal surrender would occur in Skeleton Canyon, about 60 miles south of Fort Bowie in the Arizona Territory, and a couple of days later the entire force began moving north towards the U.S. border. After the first day's travel, Aguirre and his force of about 200 Mexican troops approached the U.S. camp and demanded that the Chiricahuas be handed over to the Mexicans for "punishment." Lawton refused, but at Aguirre's insistence, a meeting between a small group of Mexicans and the Chiricahuas was arranged.

By managing to evade thousands of American and Mexican troops for about a year, Geronimo had turned himself into a legendary, almost mythical figure whose name struck fear in the hearts of white settlers across the Southwest. Even then, settlers were referring to him as "the worst Indian who ever lived." His group also represented one of the last groups of Native Americans to refuse the American settlement of their native lands in the West.

Geronimo (far right) with three warriors, 1886

Prisoners of War. Geronimo is third from right

Upon the surrender of Geronimo in 1886, the Apache Wars were truly over, and the entire Chiricahua Apache tribe (as well as Warm Springs band) was evacuated from the Southwest and held as prisoners-of-war in Florida, Alabama, and finally, Fort Sill, Oklahoma. With no leaders willing to assume Geronimo's campaign of resistance, the various Apache groups thought it in their best interest not to incur additional wrath from the U. S. government. For its part, rather than risk a resurgent uprising, the federal government thought it in their best interest not to amass all the Chiricahua Apache at Fort Sill until after Geronimo had died.

Online Resources

Other books about Native American tribes by Charles River Editors

Bibliography

Ball, Eve, "The Apache Scouts: A Chiricahua Appraisal" in *Arizona and the West*, Vol. 7, No. 4 (Winter 1965)

Ball, Eve, *In the Days of Victorio: Recollections of a Warm Springs Apache* (University of Arizona Press, Tucson, 1970)

Ball, Eve, with Nora Henn and Lynda Sanchez, *Indeh: An Apache Odyssey* (Brigham Young University Press, Provo, Utah, 1980)

Basso, Keith (editor) from the notes of Grenville Goodwin, *Western Apache Raiding and Warfare* (University of Arizona Press, Tucson, 1971)

Betzinez, Jason, with Wilber Sturtevant Nye, *I Fought with Geronimo* (The Stackpole Company, New York, 1959)

Chamberlain, Kathleen, *Victorio: Apache Warrior and Chief* (University of Oklahoma Press, Norman, 2007)

Colwell-Chanthaphonh, Chip, "Western Apache Oral Histories and Traditions of the Camp Grant Massacre" in *The American Indian Quarterly*, Volume 27, Number 3&4, Summer/Fall 2003

Crook, George, *General George Crook: His Autobiography* (University of Oklahoma Press, Norman, 1946)

Dunlay, Tom, *Kit Carson & The Indians* (University of Nebraska Press, Lincoln, 2000)

Geronimo, with S.M. Barrett, ed., *Geronimo: His Own Story* (Ballantine Books, New York,

1971)

Johnson, David, *Final report on the Battle of Cieneguilla : a Jicarilla Apache victory over the U.S. Dragoons, March 30, 1854* (U.S. Dept. of Agriculture, Forest Service, Southwestern Region, Archaeological Report Series No. 20, Albuquerque, 2009)

Pettis, George Henry, *Kit Carson's Fight with the Comanche and Kiowa Indians at the Adobe Walls* (Providence: Rider, 1878; rpt., Santa Fe, 1908)

Radbourne, Allan, "The Battle for Apache Pass: Reports of the California Volunteers" in *The Brand Book*, Vol. 34, No. 2, Spring 2001 (The English Westerners Society, London, 2001)

Rajtar, Steve, *Indian War Sites: A Guidebook to Battlefields, Monuments, and Memorials* (McFarland & Company, Inc., Jefferson, North Carolina, 1999)

Secoy, Frank, *Changing Military Patterns on the Great Plains* (American Ethnological Society, Monograph No. 21, J. J. Augustin, Locust Valley, NY, 1953)

Stevens, Robert, "The Apache Menace in Sonora, 1831-1849", in *Arizona and the West*, Vol. 6, No. 3, Autumn 1964

Thrapp, Dan, *The Conquest of Apacheria* (University of Oklahoma Press, Norman, 1975)

Utley, Robert, *Frontier Regulars: The United States Army and the Indian, 1866-1891* (Macmillan Publishing Company, New York, 1973)

Walker, Harry, "Soldier in the California Column: The Diary of John W. Teal", in *Arizona and the West*, Vol. 13, No. 1, Spring 1971

Williams, Jack, and Robert Hoover, *Arms of the Apacheria: A Comparison of Apachean and Spanish Fighting Techniques in the later 18th Century*. Katunob: Occasional Publications in Mesoamerican Anthropology, No. 25. (University of Northern Colorado, Greeley, 1983)